A Note From Rick Renner

I am on a personal quest to see a "revival of the Bible" so people can establish their lives on a firm foundation that will stand strong and endure the test when the end-time storm winds begin to intensify.

In order to experience a revival of the Bible in your personal life, it is important to take time each day to read, receive, and apply its truths to your life. James tells us that if we will continue in the perfect law of liberty — refusing to be forgetful hearers but determined to be doers — we will be blessed in our ways. As you watch or listen to the programs in this series and work through this corresponding study guide, I trust that you will search the Scriptures and allow the Holy Spirit to help you hear something new from God's Word that applies specifically to your life. I encourage you to be a doer of the Word that He reveals to you. Whatever the cost, I assure you — it will be worth it.

> Thy words were found, and I did eat them;
> and thy word was unto me the joy and rejoicing of mine heart:
> for I am called by thy name, O Lord God of hosts.
> — Jeremiah 15:16

Your brother and friend in Jesus Christ,

Rick Renner

Starting the New Year Strong

Copyright © 2020 by Rick Renner
8316 E. 73rd St.
Tulsa, Oklahoma 74133

Published by Rick Renner Ministries
www.renner.org

ISBN 13: 978-1-68031-810-4

eBook ISBN 13: 978-1-68031-811-1

How To Use This Study Guide

This five-lesson study guide corresponds to *"Starting the New Year Strong" With Rick Renner* (Renner TV). Each lesson in this study guide covers a topic that is addressed during the program series, with questions and references supplied to draw you deeper into your own private study of the Scriptures on this subject.

To derive the most benefit from this study guide, consider the following:

First, watch or listen to the program prior to working through the corresponding lesson in this guide. (Programs can also be viewed at **renner.org** by clicking on the Media/Archives links.)

Second, take the time to look up the scriptures included in each lesson. Prayerfully consider their application to your own life.

Third, use a journal or notebook to make note of your answers to each lesson's Study Questions and Practical Application challenges.

Fourth, invest specific time in prayer and in the Word of God to consult with the Holy Spirit. Write down the scriptures or insights He reveals to you.

Finally, take action! Whatever the Lord tells you to do according to His Word, do it.

For added insights on this subject, it is recommended that you obtain Rick Renner's book *Promotion: Ten Guidelines To Help You Achieve Your Long-Awaited Promotion*. You may also select from Rick's other resources by placing your order at **renner.org** or by calling 1-800-742-5593.

TOPIC

Remember

SCRIPTURES

1. **Hebrews 10:32** — But call to remembrance the former days, in which, after ye were illuminated...
2. **Hebrews 10:32 (*NIV*)** — Remember those earlier days after you had received the light...
3. **Proverbs 29:18** — Where there is no vision, the people perish...
4. **Acts 26:16-19** — But rise, and stand upon thy feet: for I have appeared unto thee for this purpose, to make thee a minister and a witness both of these things which thou hast seen, and of those things in the which I will appear unto thee; delivering thee from the people, and from the Gentiles, unto whom now I send thee, to open their eyes, and to turn them from darkness to light, and from the power of Satan unto God, that they may receive forgiveness of sins, and inheritance among them which are sanctified by faith that is in me. ...I was not disobedient unto the heavenly vision.
5. **Philippians 3:12** — Not as though I had already attained, either were already perfect: but I follow after, if that I may apprehend that for which also I am apprehended of Christ Jesus.

GREEK WORDS

1. "disobedient" — ἀπειθής (*apeithes*): unpersuadable, uncontrollable, or unleadable; Paul was not disobedient and unleadable
2. "heavenly vision" — οὐρανίῳ ὀπτασίᾳ (*ouranio optasia*): the root word οὐράνιος (*ouranios*) means originating in heaven; the word ὀπτασία (*optasia*) depicts a supernatural vision; together, it is a supernatural vision that originated in Heaven
3. "I follow" — διώκω (*dioko*): to hunt, chase, or pursue; denotes the actions of a hunter who followed after an animal in order to apprehend, to capture to kill it; like a hunter, to strategically follow after an object, principle, person, or reward until it is captured

SYNOPSIS

The five lessons in this study on *Starting the New Year Strong* will focus on the following topics:

- Remember
- Review and Be Honest
- Report and Be Honest
- Revise
- Restructure and Focus on the Future

The emphasis of this lesson:

The first step to starting the new year strong is to purposely recall to your remembrance the vision God has given you for your life. Keeping God's calling in front of you fills your heart and mind with purpose and meaning. It motivates you to move toward to fulfill your destiny.

There is tremendous value in taking time to reflect on what God has called us to do. Whether we are raising children or running a multi-million dollar business, remembering our God-ordained purpose is vital to ensure that we stay on track with fulfilling our destiny and fanning the fire of our passion for Him.

Rick and Denise Renner come together with their team just before the beginning of each new year and take an honest look at all they are doing. First, they *remember* what God has called them to do. Second, they *review* the facts of what they have done in light of their God-given call. Third, they make a *report* about what they need to do to get better and continue moving in the right direction. Fourth, they determine what things they need to *revise*. And the fifth and final step they take is to *restructure* their game plan in order to successfully achieve their desired goals.

The Value of Remembering

In Hebrews 10:32, it says, "But call to remembrance the former days, in which, after ye were illuminated…." The word "illuminated" is a translation of the Greek word *photizo*, which is from where we get the word *photograph*. The word *photizo* describes *a brilliant flash of light that leaves a lasting, permanent impression.* In the context of this verse, the writer of Hebrews is instructing his readers to call to remembrance the moment in time when God spoke and gave a very clear vision of what they were to do with their lives. In fact, the vision was so illuminating (*photizo*), it was like a brilliant flash of light that made a permanent and lasting impression.

The Bible says you have to call those moments to "remembrance." This word "remembrance" is a translation of a very old Greek word that describes *a grave, a tomb, or a sepulcher; a place where things are buried.* The fact that the Greek word *photizo* is coupled with the word for a *sepulcher* tells us that many times we bury the most important moments in our lives — the times when God speaks to us and makes a permanent, lasting impression on us, giving us specific direction for why we are here and what we are to do.

The truth is, life often becomes very busy and cluttered with activities, and we get distracted and forget the things that are most important. When we forget the direction God gave us, we get derailed from what He originally called us to do. That's why the Bible says, "…Call to remembrance the former days, in which, after ye were illuminated…" (Hebrews 10:32). The *New International Version* says, "Remember those earlier days after you had received the light…." Friend, God wants you to go back to that moment when He spoke to you and refresh your memory of what He first told you to do with your life.

Ecclesiastes 3:1 says, "To every thing there is a season, and a time to every purpose under the heaven." Since you are alive and living "under Heaven," you have a purpose! In other words, you are not an accident. God brought you into this world for a specific reason, and He wants you to have a vision for your life.

The Value of a Vision

The Bible says, "Where there is no vision, the people perish…" (Proverbs 29:18). When people have no clear-cut direction or goal for which to live, they feel *purposeless*. When that hopeless feeling seizes the heart, mind, and emotions, it doesn't take long until a man or woman begins to slide into a pit of despair. This is what the Bible means when it says, *"Where there is no vision, the people perish…."*

There are several good translations of Proverbs 29:18 such as:

- "Where there is no vision, the people live purposeless, meaningless lives…."

- "Where there is no vision, the people have no sense of direction and lose their reason for living..."
- "Where there is no vision, people become lazy, dissatisfied, and sluggish..."
- "Where there is no vision, the people cast off restraint and become undisciplined and unproductive...."

Without question, people need a sense of direction. They need to know why they are here and what they are supposed to be doing. They need borders and guidelines to keep them on track and moving forward. If you look back on your own life to seasons when you had no purpose, vision, or goal for your life, you probably sank to low levels of inactivity and even laziness. It's just a fact of life that we each need something to aim for and to keep us going.

In Genesis 1:26, God put it into the heart of man to take dominion and to achieve something great with his life. When man loses that purpose — that God-birthed spark in his heart to reach out for something great and significant — he becomes dysfunctional, lazy, lethargic, and lackadaisical about life. That's why it is so important to remember the vision God has placed in your heart.

When a person has a vision before him, he has a goal to live for! It gives meaning to his existence and gives him a reason to get up in the morning. It also provides a reason to keep fighting against the odds he encounters along the way. In many ways, a vision is like a trail you can follow. Occasionally, that trail will lead you through dense forests, dry places, and even danger. But if you stay on track, that vision will ultimately lead you to God's destination for your life.

When you have a vision, you live a full and meaningful life. Likewise, a vision enables you to live with a sense of direction and a reason for living. When you have a vision, you are disciplined, diligent, hard-working, and full of energy. Furthermore, having a vision allows you to feel fruitful, productive, and satisfied with your life.

What Is a Vision?

Have you ever wondered what a vision is? It's a good thing to ponder. The word "vision" in Hebrew means *to see*. It is the idea of having a mental image so sharp and so clear that you are able to "picture" something in your mind. This is not an abstract idea you can't latch on to. It is a concept so concrete that you can grab hold of it and say, *"That's it! I see it! I know exactly what I'm supposed to be doing with my life."*

When you have received a real vision for your life from God, you have a mental picture of what you are supposed to be doing with your life. This heavenly enlightenment also provides a sense of direction, helping you discern day by day, and even moment by moment, what you are to say yes to and what you are to say no to. As a rule, any activity or commitment that does not fit within the overall vision of your life is a distraction you need to avoid. Again, this is why it is so important to know God's vision for your life and keep it in front of you.

For example, God called Rick and Denise to broadcast the Word of God in the former Soviet Union on television into as many homes and regions as possible. When God spoke to Rick, he was able to "see" what God was asking him to do. It wasn't just an obscure idea; it was a dream that he could literally see in his mind and understand. And because he could visualize what God was calling him to do, he was able to stand on it and move forward with confidence as he traveled all over the former Soviet Union to negotiate TV contracts with former communist leaders.

What is interesting about the Hebrew word for "vision" is that it is the same root for the word *provision*. Thus, when you have a vision, you are not only able to see something, you also have a provision of direction, motivation, guidance, and power to achieve your purpose.

The Vision for the Apostle Paul

In the book of Acts, we find that God gave the apostle Paul a vision for his life the day he got saved on the road to Damascus. The Bible says that Jesus spoke to Paul and said, "But rise, and stand upon thy feet: for I have appeared unto thee for this purpose, to make thee a minister and a witness both of these things which thou hast seen, and of those things in the which I will appear unto thee; delivering thee from the people, and from the Gentiles, unto whom now I send thee, to open their eyes, and to turn them from darkness to light, and from the power of Satan unto God, that they may receive forgiveness of sins, and inheritance among them which are sanctified by faith that is in me" (Acts 26:16-18).

In this passage of Scripture, Paul recalled the vision Jesus gave him for his life, and it included some very specific things:

- He was to be a minister (Acts 26:16).

- His ministry would be filled with supernatural revelation (Acts 26:16).

- His ministry was to the Gentiles (Acts 26:17).

- God would use him to open the eyes of the Gentiles to the truth, turning them from darkness to light and from the power of Satan to the power of God (Acts 26:18).

- Through Paul, the Gentiles would receive forgiveness of sins and an inheritance among the saints (Acts 26:18).

This vision was concrete and very clear in the mind of the apostle Paul. He understood what Christ had called him to do and said, "…I was not disobedient unto the heavenly vision" (Acts 26:19). The word "disobedient" is the Greek word *apeithes*, which means *unpersuadable, uncontrollable, or unleadable*. Hence, Paul was *not* disobedient — he was *not* unleadable or unpersuadable.

The phrase "heavenly vision" is also very important. In Greek, it is *ouranio optasia*. The word *ouranio* means *originating in heaven*, and the word *optasia* depicts *a supernatural vision*. When these two words are put together, it describes *a supernatural vision that originated in Heaven*. The use of these words lets us know that what Paul heard from the lips of Jesus in Acts 26:16-18 were not a figment of his imagination or something he dreamed up. They were a divine blueprint for Paul's life that originated in Heaven.

Paul went on to say in Philippians 3:12, "Not as though I had already attained, either were already perfect: but I follow after, if that I may apprehend that for which also I am apprehended of Christ Jesus." Notice the phrase "I follow." It is the Greek term *dioko*, which means *to hunt, chase, or pursue*. It denotes *the actions of a hunter who followed after an animal in order to apprehend, to capture, or to kill it*. By using this word, Paul was saying he was like a hunter, strategically and aggressively following after God's plan for his life. He wasn't just sitting around wishing and hoping things would unfold in his favor. He had caught the scent of the vision God had for his life, and he was going after that vision with all of his might.

In lesson two, we will explore the next vital step in starting the new year strong, which is to make an *honest review* of the facts in order to move forward in greater effectiveness.

STUDY QUESTIONS

Study to shew thyself approved unto God, a workman that needeth
not to be ashamed, rightly dividing the word of truth.
— 2 Timothy 2:15

1. What does Psalm 77:11 and 12 say about remembering the things God has done?

2. Recall some of the amazing ways God has moved in your life. How has He miraculously protected you and your family, as well as provided for you, healed you, and given you undeserved mercy and favor?

3. How does remembering the goodness of God in your life light a fresh fire of hope for His involvement in what you are presently going through?

PRACTICAL APPLICATION

But be ye doers of the word, and not hearers only,
deceiving your own selves.
— James 1:22

1. Do you know what God has called you to do? Have you experienced a *photizo* (illuminating) moment when He gave you a clear vision for your life? Take a few moments to briefly describe this vision as best as you understand it. If you don't know God's calling for your life, take time now to pray and ask the Holy Spirit to reveal it to you.

2. Basically, the assignments God gives us can be placed in three categories: *daily* assignments (moment-by-moment); *seasonal* (weekly, monthly, or over a few years); and a *lifelong* assignment. Stop and think:

3. *What has God asked me to do **in the last few days**? Have I done it?*

4. *What has God assigned me to do **in this season**? Am I doing it?*

5. *What is my **life's calling**? How am I actively involved in fulfilling my destiny?*

6. When we lose our vision for what God has called us to do, we often feel *dissatisfied* with life. Has this happened to you? Are you frustrated, disappointed, and discontented with life? If so, are you still on track with what God has called you to do? If you have gotten off track,

what adjustments do you need to make to get moving in the right direction again?

TOPIC

Review and Be Honest

SCRIPTURES

1. **Hebrews 10:32** — But call to remembrance the former days, in which, after ye were illuminated...

2. **Hebrews 10:32 (*NIV*)**— Remember those earlier days after you had received the light...

3. **Proverbs 29:18** — Where there is no vision, the people perish...

4. **Habakkuk 2:2** — ...Write the vision, and make it plain upon tables, that he may run that readeth it.

5. **Acts 26:16-19** — But rise, and stand upon thy feet: for I have appeared unto thee for this purpose, to make thee a minister and a witness both of these things which thou hast seen, and of those things in the which I will appear unto thee; delivering thee from the people, and from the Gentiles, unto whom now I send thee, to open their eyes, and to turn them from darkness to light, and from the power of Satan unto God, that they may receive forgiveness of sins, and inheritance among them which are sanctified by faith that is in me. ...I was not disobedient unto the heavenly vision.

6. **Philippians 3:12,13** — Not as though I had already attained, either were already perfect: but I follow after, if that I may apprehend that for which also I am apprehended of Christ Jesus. Brethren, I count not myself to have apprehended...

7. **Proverbs 24:3 (*TLB*)** — Any enterprise is built by wise planning, becomes strong through common sense, and profits wonderfully by keeping abreast of the facts.

8. **Ecclesiastes 10:18** — By much slothfulness the building decayeth; and through idleness of the hands the house droppeth through.

9. **Proverbs 27:23** — Be thou diligent to know the state of thy flocks, and look well to thy herds.

GREEK WORDS

1. "disobedient" — ἀπειθής (*apeithes*): unpersuadable, uncontrollable, or unleadable; Paul was not disobedient and unleadable

2. "heavenly vision" — οὐρανίῳ ὀπτασίᾳ (*ouranio optasia*): the root word οὐράνιος (*ouranios*) means originating in heaven; the word ὀπτασία (*optasia*) depicts a supernatural vision; together, it is a supernatural vision that originated in Heaven

3. "I follow" — διώκω (*dioko*): to hunt, chase, or pursue; denotes the actions of a hunter who followed after an animal in order to apprehend, to capture to kill it; like a hunter, to strategically follow after an object, principle, person, or reward until it is captured

4. "already" — ἤδη (*ede*): now; already; at this present moment

5. "attained" — ἔλαβον(*elabon*): form of λαμβάνω (*lambano*); here, to have already received, yet whatever it is must be forcefully laid hold of to take into possession

6. "perfect" — τετελείωμαι (*teteleiomai*): from τελειόω (*teleioo*); here, meaning to have already reached the end game; to have already reached the end stage; to have already reached the final phase; in context, implies there is still work to be done before everything ahead is consummated

7. "apprehend" — καταλαμβάνω (*katalambano*): future tense: to seize; to grab hold of; to pull down; to tackle; to conquer; to master; to hold under one's power

8. "apprehended" — καταλαμβάνω (*katalambano*): past tense: seized; grabbed hold of; pulled down; tackled; conquered; mastered; held under Christ's power

9. "by" — ὑπὸ (*hupo*): pictures a fierce laying hold of; a masterful grip

10. "count" — λογίζομαι (*logidzomai*): to mathematically count, calculate, or tabulate; to make a logical conclusion; used in the bookkeeping world to portray a balance sheet or a profit-and-loss statement that bookkeepers prepared at the end of the month or year

SYNOPSIS

Paul Renner started serving at Rick Renner Ministries between 1987 and 1988. Leonid Bondarenko, who was one of the very first employees, came to work with the ministry when the Renners first moved to the Soviet Union in 1992. Then there is Andrey Vasilyev, who began serving as the administrator of the ministry in the year 2000, and Yura Ruls, who oversees the media department. Collectively, Rick and Denise Renner and their team members have more than 218 years of experience in their ministry to the former Soviet Union and their outreaches to the world.

Yet, with all their experience, they still take time every year to meet together to remember God's original calling on their lives and to review what they are doing as a ministry. After several weeks of introspection and planning, they all come together to review what has taken place in their area of ministry. These reviews are often filled with exciting and glorious victories. But sometimes they include notes on the efforts that did not turn out as planned.

If you are going to stay on-track and be effective at what God has called you to do, you are going to need to include a regular review of your activities. Choosing to review your progress — or lack of progress — is one of the wisest decisions you can make to help you determine how well you are progressing toward fulfilling God's vision for your life.

The emphasis of this lesson:

To stay on track and be effective in what God has called you to do, it is essential to make an honest review of yourself and your situations on a regular basis. By staying well-informed of the facts and monitoring your progress, you can know where you are and how to chart a course to where you need to be.

A Brief Review of Lesson 1

In Lesson 1, we focused on the first step to starting the new year strong, which is to *remember* the vision God gave you. In Hebrews 10:32, the Bible says, "But call to remembrance the former days, in which, after ye were illuminated...." This same verse in the *New International Version* says, "Remember those earlier days after you had received the light...."

The word "illuminated" and the word "light" are a translation of the Greek word *photizo*, which is from where we get the word *photograph*. It describes *a brilliant flash of light that leaves a lasting, permanent impression.* Here it depicts *a revelation* of truth that God spoke, which provides a very clear vision of the purpose for your life. In fact, the vision was so illuminating (*photizo*), it was like a brilliant flash of light that made a permanent and lasting impression on you.

Make no mistake — your life is not an accident. You are not here just to go to work, come home, eat, and take up space. God brought you into this world to do something special. The Bible says, "Each person is given something to do that shows who God is: Everyone gets in on it, everyone benefits" (1 Corinthians 12:7 *MSG*). The moment you realize what God has called you to do is the moment you leave a black and white world and enter a world that is a spectrum of full color. That is, everything really comes alive when you understand why you're here and what you're supposed to do.

How important is having this vision for your life? Proverbs 29:18 says, "Where there is no vision, the people perish...." When you have an illumination (*photizo*), you have vision for your life. In Hebrew, the word "vision" describes *something you can really see.* Thus, when God gives you a vision for your life, you are able *to see* what you are supposed to be doing in the present or in the future. A true vision from God is not abstract; it is clear.

What is equally interesting is that the Hebrew word for "vision" also carries the idea of *provision.* This means that when you have vision, it provides you with a sense of direction and helps you know what you should say *yes* to and what you should say *no* to. Moreover, it reveals where you should and shouldn't spend your money and where you should and shouldn't invest your time. When you're able to see what you're supposed to be doing, you are provided with guidelines, borders, and the discipline you need to move forward and accomplish your God-ordained destiny.

In Habakkuk 2:2, God said, "...Write the vision, and make it plain upon tables, that he may run that readeth it." Do you remember what God has called you to do? If you don't, take time to be still in His presence and ask Him to reveal His purpose for your life once again.

Paul Had a Vision for His Life From Day One

The apostle Paul knew clearly what Jesus had called him to do, and when he had been arrested for his faith and stood before King Agrippa, he reflected on his life assignment.

The Bible says that Jesus spoke to Paul when he was on the road to Damascus and said, "...Rise, and stand upon thy feet: for I have appeared unto thee for this purpose..." (Acts 26:16). The moment Paul surrendered his life to the lordship of Christ, he immediately discovered his purpose.

Jesus said He appeared to Paul to make him "...a minister and a witness both of these things which thou hast seen, and of those things in the which I will appear unto thee" (Acts 26:16). From the beginning, Paul was called into fulltime ministry — a ministry filled with supernatural revelation.

Who was Paul's ministry to? Jesus said, "Delivering thee from the people, and from the Gentiles, unto whom now I send thee" (Acts 26:17). There was nothing abstract about Paul's calling. He was sent by Jesus to reach the Gentiles with the Gospel. Paul would be used "to open their eyes, and to turn them from darkness to light, and from the power of Satan unto God, that they may receive forgiveness of sins, and inheritance among them which are sanctified by faith that is in [Jesus]" (Acts 26:18).

Paul's vision was very clear, and it became a trail he could follow to fulfill his destiny. In Acts 26:19, he declared with great confidence to King Agrippa, "...I was not disobedient unto the heavenly vision." We saw that the phrase "heavenly vision" describes *a supernatural vision that originated in Heaven*. Paul said he was not "disobedient" to the supernatural vision Jesus gave him, which means he was *not unpersuadable or unleadable*. He willingly submitted to the guidance and leading of the Holy Spirit and worked tirelessly to fulfill his destiny.

Paul Took Time To Review His Progress

Once you have taken time to "remember" the vision God has called you to carry out, the next step is to press pause on your activities and *review* the facts of what you have achieved. That is what Paul chose to do, and it is recorded in Philippians 3:12. He told the Philippian believers, "Not as though I had already attained, either were already perfect: but I follow after, if that I may apprehend that for which also I am apprehended of Christ Jesus."

There are several important words to understand in this verse, including the word "already." It is the Greek word *ede*, which means *now; already*; or *at this present moment*. Paul was looking at the present moment he was in, reviewing how well he was fulfilling the vision Jesus had given him for his life. In that moment, he said that he had not "already attained" what he had been called to, nor was he, "already perfect."

The word "attained" is the Greek word *elabon*, which is a form of the word *lambano*. Here, it means *to have already received*, yet whatever it is must be forcefully laid hold of to take into one's possession. The word "perfect" in Greek is *teteleiomai*, which means *to have already reached the end game; to have already reached the end stage*; or *to have already reached the final phase*. In context here, it implies there is still work to be done before everything ahead is consummated.

Basically, Paul said, "I've done a lot, but I've not done everything. I've not come to the end of my race; there's still a great deal of work to be done before everything can be wrapped up." Again, at that particular moment in Paul's life, he took time to really look at his life and review what he had accomplished in light of the vision Christ had spoken to him on the day he was saved.

Paul Had Not Fully 'Apprehended' The Vision Jesus Gave Him for His Life

Once Paul realized he had not fully completed the call on his life, he said, "…I follow after, if that I may apprehend that for which also I am apprehended of Christ Jesus" (Philippians 3:12).

The phrase "I follow" is the Greek word *dioko*, which is a hunting term that means *to hunt, chase, or pursue*. It denotes *the actions of a hunter who followed after an animal in order to apprehend, to capture, or to kill it*. Like a hunter, the word *dioko* means *to strategically follow after an object, principle, person, or reward until it is captured*. Paul's use of the word *dioko* in this verse is the equivalent of him saying, "I have not achieved everything I've been called to do, so I'm going to put on my hunting clothes and begin to follow after and track down the vision God gave me for my life. And I'm not going to stop until I finally apprehend it."

This brings us to the words "apprehend" and "apprehended," which is the Greek word *katalambano*. The first use of *katalambano* — translated as "apprehend" — is future tense, and it means *to seize; to grab hold of; to pull down; to tackle; to conquer; to master; or to hold under one's power*. The second use of the word *katalambano* — translated as "apprehended" — is past tense, and it means *seized; grabbed hold of; pulled down; tackled; conquered; mastered;* or *held under Christ's power*.

When Paul said, "…I follow after, if that I may apprehend that for which also I am apprehended of Christ Jesus" (Philippians 3:12), he was literally saying, "I'm on a hunt *to seize, to grab hold of, to pull down, to tackle, to conquer, to master, and to hold under my power* all that Jesus has *seized me, grabbed hold of me, pulled me down, tackled me, conquered me, and mastered me for*." This is a clear picture of the attitude you need to have if you're going to finish your race and fully apprehend what God has called you to do. You can't sit and wait for your vision to fall into place and be fulfilled on its own. You have to go after it like a hunter — *dioko*.

In Prison, Paul Took Time To Review His Achievements in Light of the Calling Christ Gave Him

Paul went on to say, "Brethren, I count not myself to have apprehended…" (Philippians 3:13). Once again, we see the word "apprehended," which is the past tense of the Greek word *katalambano*, meaning *seized; grabbed hold of; pulled down; tackled; conquered; mastered;* or *to be held under Christ's power*. Also notice the word "count." It is a translation of the Greek word *logidzomai*, which means *to mathematically count, calculate,* or *tabulate*. It can also mean *to make a logical conclusion*. The word *logidzomai* was used in the bookkeeping world to portray a balance sheet or a profit-and-loss statement that bookkeepers prepared at the end of the month or year.

Keep in mind that when Paul wrote this letter to the Philippian believers he was in prison. And while he had time to think, he took advantage of the moment. Thus, when he used the word *logidzomai* — translated here as "count" — he was literally saying, "I'm going to compare the facts of what I've actually accomplished to the vision Jesus gave me for my life." In those moments, Paul took time to *remember* the calling Christ illuminated within him, and he began to compare it with what he had done. On one side of his ledger was the original vision from Jesus, which we read earlier in Acts 26:16-18, and on the other side were the achievements he had produced up until that point.

When Paul finished tabulating, he looked at the vision and then reviewed what he'd actually done, and said, "Although I've done a lot, it does not yet fully complete what I've been called to do. My calculations and my review of the facts show me that there is still more for me to do. I've come up short and count *not* myself to have apprehended everything that God has told me to do."

Paul was willing to be honest and make a very serious review of the facts. Friend, you've got to be willing to take an honest look at where you are and what you've done, and while you should be thankful for all that God has enabled you to accomplish, you need to be able to see and admit what you still need to do. If you have fallen behind or become distracted and gotten off track, ask God to forgive you and take the steps necessary to self-correct.

Stay Informed of the Facts and Be Honest With Yourself

It is clear from Scripture that anything worthwhile is going to take hard work, keen strategy, and a regular, honest evaluation of ourselves and where we are in life. Look carefully at what these verses have to say:

> **Any enterprise is built by wise planning, becomes strong through common sense, and profits wonderfully by keeping abreast of the facts.**
> **Proverbs 24:3,4 (*TLB*)**

When you keep abreast of the facts — being honest with God, yourself, and others — you will know exactly where you are in terms of growth and progress. Being ignorant of the facts is the fastest way to lose territory and to let someone else take your place.

The Bible also says:

> **By much slothfulness the building decayeth; and through idleness of the hands the house droppeth through.**
> **Ecclesiastes 10:18**

Basically, this verse says if you don't pay attention and remain actively involved, things will fall to pieces. So, stay abreast of all the facts, and be honest with yourself and others if needed. Similar wisdom is found in the book of Proverbs, which says,

Be thou diligent to know the state of thy flocks, and look well to thy herds.

Proverbs 27:23

In biblical times, flocks represented wealth and were huge investments. Essentially, this verse is saying if you want to be blessed, you have to look well to your personal business and progress (or your lack of progress). Taking an honest look at your situation will help you know where you are now and how to chart a path to where you need to be. This will require you to get honest before the Lord and take a hard look at what you're doing. Although an honest evaluation of your life isn't always fun, it's necessary to grow.

Friend, today — and the new year — can be your new beginning! You can start fresh and make a brand-new choice to do things differently from this point forward. Repent of previous poor choices you've made and receive God's help to propel you forward.

In our next lesson, we will examine how to take your review and make an honest *report* of yourself to your friends, your spouse, and your team members.

STUDY QUESTIONS

Study to shew thyself approved unto God, a workman that needeth not to be ashamed, rightly dividing the word of truth.
— 2 Timothy 2:15

1. One of the most important parts of honestly reviewing where you are is knowing what is going on inside your heart. What vital truth does God say about your heart in Jeremiah 17:9?

2. According to Jeremiah 17:10; First Chronicles 28:9; Psalm 44:21; and Proverbs 15:11, how can you really know the true condition of your heart? (Also *consider* Hebrews 4:12.)

3. As you take time to make an honest review of yourself and where you are, read Psalm 139:23 and 24, and use David's words to create a personal prayer that invites God's involvement to help you understand what's going on in your heart.

PRACTICAL APPLICATION

> But be ye doers of the word, and not hearers only,
> deceiving your own selves.
> —James 1:22

1. Like Paul, have you ever taken time to *review* your progress? Have you created a spiritual ledger (symbolically or literally) and calculated what you have actually accomplished in comparison to God's call on your life? If so, what did you learn?

2. If it's been a long time — or you can't remember the last time you took an honest look at where you are and the progress you've made — take time now to be honest with God, yourself, and others if need be and make an honest review of the facts.

3. What do the facts about yourself and your current situations tell you about where you are in terms of growth and progress? If you have fallen behind or become distracted and gotten off track, ask God to forgive you and take the steps necessary to self-correct.

LESSON 3

TOPIC

Report and Be Honest

SCRIPTURES

1. **Philippians 3:13** — Brethren, I count not myself to have apprehended: but this one thing I do, forgetting those things which are behind, and reaching forth unto those things which are before.

2. **Proverbs 24:3 (*TLB*)** — Any enterprise is built by wise planning, becomes strong through common sense, and profits wonderfully by keeping abreast of the facts.

3. **1 Corinthians 13:12** — For now we see through a glass, darkly...

GREEK WORDS

1. "count" — λογίζομαι (*logidzomai*): to mathematically count, calculate, or tabulate; to make a logical conclusion; used in the bookkeeping

world to portray a balance sheet or a profit-and-loss statement that bookkeepers prepared at the end of the month or year

2. "apprehended" — **καταλαμβάνω** (*katalambano*): past tense: seized; grabbed hold of; pulled down; tackled; conquered; mastered; held under Christ's power

3. "forgetting" — **ἐπιλανθάνομαι** (*epilanthanomai*): to turn away from and forget; to be put aside, deliberately ignored, purposefully disregarded, and completely forgotten; denotes something that may have really been true in the past, but is no longer applicable; depicts something finished, done with, or obsolete, and hence no longer applicable

4. "behind" — **ὀπίσω** (*opiso*): describes something that should be put behind; obsolete or irrelevant; something that should be relegated to the past; abandoned or left behind

5. "reaching forth" — **ἐπεκτείνομαι** (*epekteinomai*): pictures a foot racer; the image of a racer who is pressing forward so hard and is so stretched out that his entire body is arching forward as his arms reach ahead to grasp the goal before him; to strain or to stretch forward

6. "before" — **ἔμπροσθεν** (*emprosthen*): in front of you; the things set before you; what is set before the face, as opposed to what is behind your back

SYNOPSIS

To start the new year strong, we have seen that there are some specific things we need to do, such as *remembering the vision* God has given us for our lives and taking time to *honestly review the facts* of where we are and how much progress we've made toward our goals. Once these actions have been carried out, *making an honest report* is the next step.

Rick and Denise Renner are blessed with nearly 200 employees, and each year they gather together with their top team members to remember their vision, review their progress, and make an honest report of what they need to change in order to continue being as effective as they can in all their endeavors. This report lets them know what is working and should be continued, as well as what is not working and needs to be modified or stopped. It is a time of honest reflection and accountability that yields great rewards.

The emphasis of this lesson:

Once you have carefully reviewed the facts regarding where you are and what you've accomplished, the next step is to make an honest, gut-level report to see what you're doing right, what you're doing wrong, and what you need to change in order to fulfill your God-given vision.

Remember Your God-Given Vision

In our first lesson, we focused our attention on Hebrews 10:32, which says, "But call to remembrance the former days, in which, after ye were illuminated...." The word "illuminated" here is the Greek word *photizo*, and it describes *a brilliant flash of light that leaves a lasting, permanent impression.* Here it depicts the moment when God spoke to you and gave you a clear, unforgettable vision of the purpose for your life. In Hebrew, the word for "vision" describes *something you can see.* It includes the provision of direction regarding what you should and should not do, and where you should and should not go. God wants you to take time to revisit the memory of the divine moments and what He spoke to you.

Make an Honest *Review* of the Facts

The second step to starting the new year strong is to take time to honestly review where you are in order to measure how much progress you have made toward fulfilling your vision. This is what the apostle Paul learned to do, and we see an example of this in his letter to the believers in Philippi. At that point in his life, he was in prison and had a lot of time on his hands. Rather than waste those moments, Paul decided to make a review of his life.

In Philippians 3:13, Paul said, "Brethren, I count not myself to have apprehended...." We saw that the word "count" is a translation of the Greek word *logidzomai*, which means *to mathematically count, calculate, or tabulate; to make a logical conclusion.* It was a word used in the bookkeeping world to portray a balance sheet or a profit-and-loss statement that bookkeepers prepared at the end of the month or year.

Paul said, "Brethren, I count not myself to have apprehended..." (Philippians 3:13). The word "apprehended," which is used in verses 12 and 13, is the Greek word *katalambano*. It is a compound of the word *kata*, which carries the idea of *domination* or *subjection*, and the word *lambano*, which means *to take* or *to seize*. When these two words come together to form *katalambano*, it means *to seize, to grab hold of, to pull down, to tackle, to conquer, to master,* or *to hold under one's power.*

Without question, Paul had done many things to advance the Kingdom of God — possibly more than anyone else. But that didn't matter. He needed to review *his* life to see if he had accomplished what Christ had called him to do. So with time on his hands, he created a spiritual ledger and placed a description of his original calling from Jesus on one side and the facts of what he had actually achieved on the other side. When he honestly reviewed his activities, he came to the conclusion that he had *not* apprehended all that Christ had called him to do — he had *not seized, tackled, conquered, mastered,* or *grabbed hold of* everything Jesus told him to accomplish. There was still work to be done.

Always keep in mind that just because you have done more — or better — than others, it doesn't mean you've completed your calling. You're not going to be judged by how much you accomplished in comparison to others. When you stand before the Judgement Seat of Christ, He is going to ask you how well you carried out the specific call He placed on *your* life. That is why it is so important to take time to regularly review the facts of what you have done in light of your God-given vision.

Develop an Honest *Report*

Once you have reviewed the facts of where you are and what you've done, you need to *make an honest report* about your situation. This is what Rick and Denise and their ministry team do annually after they've taken time to remember their vision and make an honest review of what they're doing well and what they could do better. As they gather together, they respectfully lay everything out on the table for everyone to see. Being gut-level honest is the key to recognizing and implementing the needed adjustments.

It's essential that you take the time to recount the facts about where you are and what you've done and share it with people like your spouse, your family, your team members, or your business partners. This brings the harsh reality to the forefront where it cannot be ignored or denied. At that point, you have a choice to make: You can sweep the problems under the carpet and pretend everything is all right (when it's not). Or, you can make the decision to embrace the truth and make the necessary changes to be what God wants you to be and to achieve what He wants to give you.

Looking again at Philippians 3:13, Paul said, "Brethren, I count not myself to have apprehended: but this one thing I do, forgetting those things which are behind, and reaching forth unto those things which are before." Once Paul realized he had not finished all the work Christ had called him to do, he focused all his energies on one thing — "...forgetting those things which are behind, and reaching forth unto those things which are before."

Forget the Things Behind You

The word "forgetting" is the Greek word *epilanthanomai*, which means *to turn away from and forget*. It can also mean *to be put aside, deliberately ignored, purposefully disregarded, and completely forgotten*. This word denotes *something that may have really been true in the past, but is no longer applicable*. Furthermore, it depicts *something finished, done with, or obsolete, and hence no longer applicable*.

Paul declared he was "...forgetting — *epilanthanomai* — those things which are behind..." (Philippians 3:13). The word "behind" is the Greek word *opiso*, and it describes *something that should be put behind you*; *something obsolete or completely irrelevant*; or *something that should be relegated to the past*. It carries the idea of being *abandoned* or *left behind*.

The truth is you cannot do anything about what happened in the past. You can, however, do something about the future. Instead of wallowing in regret over wrong choices you've made or a lack of effort, Paul said, "Forget what is behind." In other words, *purposely disregard it, deliberately ignore it, put it aside as obsolete and no longer applicable* and begin focusing on the future. If you've done something wrong, like abandoning your responsibility or being lazy, repent and ask God to forgive you. If you feel prompted to do so, apologize to your spouse, your family, or your team. Then get up and get moving in the right direction.

Reach For What Is Before You

Along with forgetting the past, Paul said he was "...reaching forth unto those things which are before" (Philippians 3:13). The phrase "reaching forth" is a marvelous Greek word — the word *epekteinomai* — which is *the picture of a foot racer*. Specifically, it is *the image of a racer who is pressing forward so hard and is so stretched out that his entire body is arching forward as his arms reach ahead to grasp the goal before him*. His heart is pumping wildly and his blood vessels are bulging as everything inside of him is reaching toward his goal. The phrase "reaching forth" — the Greek word *epekteinomai* — literally means *to strain or to stretch forward.*

Like a foot racer, you have to stretch and strain forward toward your future. In order for you to fulfill your purpose, you're going to have to put forth all your energies and your very best efforts. You'll have to leave the past in the past and focus on "…those things which are before."

The word "before" is the Greek word *emprosthen*, and it describes *what is right in front of you; the things set before you; what is set before the face, as opposed to what is behind your back.* Again, you can do nothing about what is behind you; you can only deal with what is right in front of you. By all means, repent for any wrongdoing and learn from your mistakes, but then you must move forward.

Perhaps what you see right in front of your face is a mountain of problems or a huge mess on your hands. In order for you to reach forth for the things that are before you, you're going to have to face your challenges and conquer them. Although it may look impossible, you can do it!

Stay On Top of Things: Seek the Wisdom of God and Leading of His Holy Spirit

As we noted in our previous lesson, the Bible says, "Any enterprise is built by wise planning, becomes strong through common sense, and profits wonderfully by keeping abreast of the facts" (Proverbs 24:3,4 *TLB*).

To totally fulfill the vision God has given you, you have to have wise planning and common sense. If you ask God, He will give you the common sense you need to grow strong and move forward in your endeavors. And by staying abreast of the facts, you will profit greatly and know exactly where you are in terms of growth and progress.

Being ignorant of the facts is the fastest way to lose territory and to let someone else take your place. If you realize that you've done wrong and deviated from the original vision God gave you, make the choice to repent and get back on track. Once you do, God's favor and power and provision will begin to flow to you and operate in your life in powerful ways.

Realize that in this life, our vision is limited. The Bible says, "For now we see through a glass, darkly..." (1 Corinthians 13:12). When we receive our glorified bodies in Heaven and see Jesus face to face, we will see everything clearly. Until then, we need to seek the wisdom of God and rely on the supernatural insight of His Holy Spirit.

If you get distracted or make a mistake because you didn't see things as clearly as you should, don't give in to condemnation and regret. Repent, ask God to forgive you, and go on. Get quiet and still in His presence and listen for His voice of direction. If you sense Him leading you to make a revision or to sharpen your understanding in a way that changes your outlook, then it's time for you to *revise* what you're doing and go in a new direction. Friend, God wants His power to flow through you to help you fulfill the vision He placed in your heart, but you may need to revise the vision to see it happen. That is what we will focus on in our next lesson.

STUDY QUESTIONS

Study to shew thyself approved unto God, a workman that needeth not to be ashamed, rightly dividing the word of truth.
— 2 Timothy 2:15

1. What does the Bible say in Hebrews 9:27 and Romans 14:10-12 that awaits each and every person that has ever lived — both Christians and non-Christians alike?

2. According to Revelation 20:11-15, what will this day be like for non-believers who rejected salvation through Jesus, the Son of God? (Also consider Jesus' words in Matthew 11:20-24.)

3. As a believer who has put your faith in Christ, what can you expect to take place on that day? What will Jesus be examining in your life? (*See* Matthew 16:27; 2 Corinthians 5:10; Revelation 22:12.) According to Psalm 103:12 and Colossians 2:13,14, what will He *not* be looking at?

PRACTICAL APPLICATION

But be ye doers of the word, and not hearers only, deceiving your own selves.
— James 1:22

1. Have you made a wrong decision and become distracted or gotten off track from the original vision God gave you? You're in good company. Many have experienced this same dilemma, including Abraham, the father of faith, and Elijah the mighty prophet of God. Instead of wallowing in regret over a past mistake that you can't do anything about, repent, ask God to forgive you, and begin to move forward.

2. In order to successfully move forward, you must purposefully *forget the things behind you*. These include activities, memories, or ways of thinking that are *obsolete*, *irrelevant*, or *should be relegated to the past*. Right now, what things do you know you need to *turn away from*, *deliberately ignore*, and *purposefully disregard*?

3. In addition to forgetting what is behind you, God wants you "reaching forth unto the things which are before you" (Philippians 3:13). What things are in front of you that you sense God's Spirit urging you to reach for? (These are things that are related to your life's calling.)

4. The Greek word for "reaching forth" is *the image of a racer who is pressing forward so hard and is so stretched out that his entire body is arching forward to grasp the goal before him.* Be honest. Would you say this describes you? Are you putting forth all your energies and your very best efforts to apprehend what God has called you to do? If not, why?

LESSON 4

TOPIC

Revise

SCRIPTURES

1. **1 Corinthians 13:12** — For now we see through a glass, darkly; but then face to face: now I know in part; but then shall I know even as also I am known

GREEK WORDS

1. "now" — **ἄρτι** (*arti*): presently; at this present moment; here and now; right now

2. "we see" — **βλέπω** (*blepo*): to see, perceive, or discern

3. "through" — δι' (*di*): pictures one trying to peer through something
4. "glass" — ἔσοπτρον (*esoptron*): a mirror made of highly polished metal; ancient mirrors were fashioned of highly polished metal so they could not produce a clear and distinct image; to get a better image, an onlooker had to look into the mirror from several different angles; here we see an ardent student looking at revelation from different angles or standpoints to try to get a clearer image of truth; also used to depict Roman glass
5. "darkly" — αἴνιγμα (*hainigma*): something that is obscure; where we get the word "enigma"
6. "then" — τότε (*tote*): then, at that precise moment
7. "now" — ἄρτι (*arti*): presently; at this very moment
8. "I know" — γινώσκω (*ginosko*): to know, perceive, or comprehend; to recognize
9. "in part" — ἐκ μέρους (*ek merous*): partially; from parts; pieces, not the whole picture

SYNOPSIS

To run a ministry like RENNER Ministries, it takes a team of nearly 200 people, including several key leaders who oversee certain areas of outreach. For instance, Paul Renner leads the Moscow Good News Church, which is a huge responsibility. Leonid Bondarenko is in charge of data and information and has been a part of the team since 1992. Then there is Andrey Vasilyev, who is the creator and engineering director of the online church, which is growing and expanding rapidly. Yura Ruls is also a vital leader who is in charge of the Renner media company in Russia, which is called Media Mir.

To keep all these aspects of ministry humming harmoniously and advancing God's Kingdom, Rick and Denise meet with these leaders annually. As they sit together, the first thing they do is *remember* the primary vision Jesus called them to accomplish. Second, they make a very truthful *review* to the Lord, to themselves, and to each other — noting what is working, what is not working, and what they need to do better. This is a time of transparency and accountability, where gut-level honesty is required.

Once this full evaluation is laid on the table, Rick and his leaders transition into the fourth phase, which is to *revise*. This is the point where you recognize that if what you are doing to fulfill your vision is not working, you choose to change it and try something new. Rather than let pride keep you stuck in an unproductive pattern, humbling yourself and admitting you've made a mistake is the best thing you can do to get back on track and begin heading in the right direction.

The emphasis of this lesson:

Once you've made an honest report of where you are and how well you're progressing toward achieving your vision, the next step is to revise. Rather than continue with methods that aren't working, you are to prayerfully seek new, more effective ways of making your vision become a reality.

A REVIEW OF WHAT WE'VE LEARNED

Step 1: *Remember* Your God-Given Vision

In our first lesson, we examined Hebrews 10:32, which says, "But call to remembrance the former days, in which, after ye were illuminated...." We learned that the word "illuminated" is the Greek word *photizo*, which describes *a brilliant flash of light that leaves a lasting, permanent impression.* This verse refers to the moment God spoke to you and gave you a clear vision of your calling in life. It is vital that you remember and never forget what God has called you to do. Remembering will help protect you from becoming distracted and deviating from your divine destiny. For more on what it means to *remember*, please refer back to Lesson 1.

Step 2: Make an Honest *Review* of the Facts

The second step to starting the new year strong is to take time to honestly *review* where you are so you can measure how much progress you've made toward fulfilling your vision. This includes determining what you're doing right and what you're doing wrong — the habits that have been productive and those that have been unproductive. To accomplish your divine destiny, you have to be willing to take an honest look at where you are and what you've done, and while you should be thankful for all that God has enabled you to accomplish, you also need to be able to see and admit what you still need to do. If you've fallen behind or become distracted and gotten off track, ask God to forgive you and take the steps necessary to self-correct. For more on the importance of *review*, please refer back to Lesson 2.

Step 3: Make an Honest *Report*

Once you have taken time to carefully review the facts and have seen where you're still on track and where you have veered from your original vision, the next step is to make an honest *report*. When you make a report, you get blatantly honest with those you are working with, laying all the cards on the table to collectively examine what's right, what's wrong, and what needs to change. An honest report helps you and everyone else see what needs to be revised in order to reach your desired goals. For more on how to make an honest *report*, please refer back to Lesson 3.

Everyone Makes Mistakes

Have you ever sincerely thought you knew what God wanted you to do, but you later found out that you were mistaken? That's actually quite normal. There are people all throughout Scripture who have experienced this dilemma, including Abraham — the "father of faith."

God spoke to him clearly and said, "…Get thee out of thy country, and from thy kindred, and from thy father's house, unto a land that I will show thee" (Genesis 12:1). God's directions were simple: "I want you and your wife, by yourselves, to leave your country, your family, and your father's home and follow Me into a new land." Well, Abraham was willing to leave his country and follow God, but his father was up in age and he had a nephew from his deceased brother that he felt responsible for. Thus, when God spoke these directions to Abraham, it is very possible he got confused and thought, *God, do you really want me to leave my elderly father? Do You really want me to abandon my nephew Lot? Surely this would be irresponsible.*

In light of Abraham's actions, we can see that he added his own under-standing to what the Lord had said. Instead of it just being him and Sarah making the journey, he brought his father, his nephew, and all of his servants. Unfortunately, the extra people became an overwhelming responsibility that he had to contend with as he tried to answer God's call on his life. His actions caused a real disruption and a delay in God's plan. Eventually, Abraham had to be confronted by his mistake and revise his game plan to get back on track.

The truth is everyone makes mistakes — *everyone*. We make the best decisions we know to make, but from time to time, we misunderstand and misinterpret our situations and what we believe God is telling us to do, and we end up veering off course. When this happens, it is better to humble yourself, admit you were wrong, and get back on track with God's plan. It's foolish to stick with the old, wrong plan just because you're too embarrassed to admit you made a mistake. Humility paves the way for Gods power to flow in and through your life.

All of Us Have Blurred Vision

Now, you may be thinking, *Why do we make these kinds of mistakes?* The apostle Paul answers this question in First Corinthians 13:12. Under the anointing of the Holy Spirit, he wrote:

> **For now we see through a glass, darkly; but then face to face: now I know in part; but then shall I know even as also I am known.**

In this verse, Paul identifies a spiritual handicap that *every* believer has — *blurred vision.* This means our understanding right now is not as clear as it will be when we see Jesus face to face. Until that time, it's just a fact that we'll occasionally make mistakes and do things that aren't entirely correct — simply because we're not able to see the full picture. Let's unpack the original meaning of some key words in this verse to really grasp what God is communicating.

'For now we see through...'

One of the first words in this passage is the word "now." It is the Greek word *arti*, and it means *presently, at this present moment, here and now,* or *right now.* Paul is speaking specifically of our present life on earth, which is temporary and will one day come to an end.

He said, "For now we see through...." The words "we see" is a translation of the Greek word *blepo,* which means *to see, perceive, or discern.* The word "through" is from the Greek word *di,* and it pictures *one trying to peer through something that is hard to see through.*

'A glass darkly'

Specifically, Paul said what we are trying to see through is "a glass darkly." What's interesting is that the word "glass" does not refer to a clear window pane you are likely imagining. The word "glass" is the word *esoptron,* which is an old Greek word describing *a mirror made of highly polished metal.* In the ancient world, mirrors were not the kind of mirrors we have today.

They were fashioned of highly polished metal. Consequently, they could not produce a clear and distinct image. To get a better image, the viewer had to look into the mirror from several different angles. The use of the word *esoptron* — translated here as "glass" — depicts an ardent student looking at revelation from several different angles or standpoints to try to get a clearer image of truth.

But that is not the only thing this word *esoptron* — glass — communicates. It was also used to describe Roman glass. During the First Century, which is the time this passage was written, the color of Roman glass was very beautiful, but it was also quite flawed. In fact, to look through Roman glass, you might see light on the other side, but you would not see a distinct image.

Hence, the apostle Paul used this word to tell us that we are very limited in our understanding — that sometimes it's like us holding a hand mirror of highly polished metal trying to get clear understanding. We can see an image, but it's not distinct. In fact, we have to look at it from several different angles in order to get a real image of truth. Although the revelation is there, you can't always see it clearly.

Think about who wrote this passage of Scripture — the apostle Paul. This is the man who had been given tremendous insight and revelation concerning Christ, the Church, the rapture, and spiritual warfare. It is the same man who wrote most of the books of the New Testament. Even *he* had the handicap of blurred vision and was limited in his ability to see spiritually.

This brings us to the word "darkly," which is the Greek word *hainigma*. It describes *something that is obscure*; it is where we get the word "enigma," which is the word for *a mystery* or *a riddle*. If we take the meanings of these words together, it lets us know that our spiritual vision and understanding is going to be blurry and inaccurate from time to time, and it will remain that way until we see Jesus face to face.

Our Spiritual Vision: 'Now' vs. 'Then'

Paul went on to say, "…Now I know in part; but then shall I know even as also I am known" (1 Corinthians 13:12). First, he reiterates the fact that our present understanding is limited by saying, "Now I know in part."

The word "now" is once again the Greek word *arti*, meaning *presently*; *at this present moment*; *here and now*; or *right now*. For the second time in the same verse, Paul is speaking explicitly of our present, temporary life on earth.

He then adds the word "then," which is the Greek word *tote*, meaning *then*, *at that precise moment*. This word refers specifically to the moment when we're going to see Jesus face to face. In that instant, all obscurity will evaporate and we will see and understand everything clearly for the first time.

In fact, Paul said, "...Then shall I know..." (1 Corinthians 13:12). The phrase "I know" is a form of the Greek word *ginosko*, which means *to know, perceive, or comprehend*; *to recognize*. Right now there are certain things we know and comprehend about God and His ways. For example, we know that God is a God of healing — one of His names is Jehovah Rapha, which means *the Lord heals*. We also know that it is God's will that His children are prosperous (*see* 3 John 2). Although we have general knowledge of these and many other aspects of God's character, many times we don't understand how to activate these attributes in our lives.

Why is this the case? Paul said it is because, "...Now we know in part..." (1 Corinthians 13:12). The words "in part" is the Greek word *ek merous*, which means *partially* or *from parts*. It denotes *pieces, not the whole picture*. The best illustration of the words "in part" would be a jigsaw puzzle. Can you see one in your mind's eye? On the cover of the box is a beautiful-ly-colored picture, but when that cover is removed, the image is broken up into hundreds of tiny pieces. In many ways, this is a reflection of our understanding of who God is. Each experience we walk through in life with Him is like a piece of that puzzle. When He reveals a facet of who He is and who we are in Him, we are able to see a little bit more of the "big picture" of Him. For us to see the whole picture, all the pieces need to be in place. That *will* happen the day we see Jesus face to face. Until then, we know Him "in part."

Even the apostle Paul — with all the "pieces of the puzzle" he had from his life of devotion to God — could only see God "through a glass darkly." The same is true for us. The "glass" we are looking through to see and understand who God is has flaws. It is like highly polished metal that we are looking at from multiple vantage points trying to get an accurate glimpse of God. No matter how hard we try, there will always be things we don't fully understand and times we misinterpret things. Although this truth may seem to be discouraging, it is actually quite liberating. It provides peace of mind to the perfectionist and freedom from the haunting fear of making a wrong decision.

How Does All This Apply to You?

Let's take all of what we've learned so far about starting the new year strong and fulfilling God's will for your life and see how it applies to you. First of all, you know from Scripture God's general will for your life. And you probably have also experienced a *photizo* moment when God spoke to you, and you were illuminated with an image of His divine destiny for your life. The Bible urges you to remember it and never ever forget it. If you've allowed your vision to become buried along the way, it's time for you to unearth it and set it back in front of you as a monument that is always in sight.

Then, you need to make a review of where you are and what progress you have made toward fulfilling that vision. Once you complete your review, your next step is to make an honest report of all you've discovered. This report is a gut-level, honest appraisal that reveals what you're doing right, what you're doing wrong, what methods are working, what methods are not working, and where you need to improve. This report is to be shared with people like your spouse, your family, your friends, your team, or those with whom you're working and doing life.

If you discover that you've gotten off track or you misunderstood something the Lord said to you, don't feel condemned. Making mistakes is a part of life that everyone experiences — even people like Abraham and Paul. Rather than wallow in regret and remorse or perpetuate your mistake by continuing to do what you know is not working, repent and receive God's forgiveness and get back on track. If necessary, go to those you are serving with and say, "Hey, I've made a mistake. It's time for us to revise." Yes, it might be a bit humbling to do, but it is the humble who receive God's empowering grace (*see* James 4:6).

If God has helped you better understand the assignment He has given you, prayerfully revise the way you're carrying things out. Once that revision is written down and understood by everyone, the next step you need to take is to *restructure* to produce the growth God wants to give you. This will be the focus of our final lesson.

STUDY QUESTIONS

**Study to shew thyself approved unto God, a workman that needeth
not to be ashamed, rightly dividing the word of truth.**
— 2 Timothy 2:15

1. The Bible is filled with people who made sincere mistakes. What
made them great was that they repented, got back on track, and finished the race God had for them. If you have fallen, don't stay down.
Repent and get up and get moving in the right direction — this is
God's will for you. Take time to read and write out **First John 1:9** and
the first part of **Proverbs 24:16** to help seal this truth deep in your
heart.

2. When you think about people in Scripture who made mistakes,
repented, and changed course, who comes to mind? How does their
example give you hope that God is not mad at you and you can still
fulfill your calling in life?

PRACTICAL APPLICATION

But be ye doers of the word, and not hearers only,
deceiving your own selves.
— James 1:22

1. Rick shared how there have been several times in his life when he
thought he knew what God wanted him to do, but he misunderstood
God's instructions. Can you think of a similar situation in your own
life? If so, briefly describe what took place. In light of what you have
learned in this lesson, how do you see the situation differently?

2. Think back to a mistake you made because you couldn't see the full
picture. Do you still feel guilty and condemned because of your
choices? How does this lesson change your perspective of that situation (and others like it)? How does it encourage you to receive God's
mercy and grace? (*See* Hebrews 4:15,16.)

3. How does this understanding help you have more mercy and patience
for others when they make mistakes?

4. First Corinthians 13:12 tells us that in this life, we see things
"through a glass darkly" and only understand things "in part." Now
that you know you're only accountable for the "pieces" and "parts" that
God reveals to you, how does this change what you expect of yourself?

TOPIC

Restructure and Focus on the Future

SCRIPTURES

1. **1 Corinthians 13:12** — For now we see through a glass, darkly; but then face to face: now I know in part; but then shall I know even as also I am known.

2. **Philippians 3:13-15** — Brethren, I count not myself to have apprehended: but this one thing I do, forgetting those things which are behind, and reaching forth unto those things which are before, I press toward the mark for the prize of the high calling of God in Christ Jesus. Let us therefore, as many as be perfect, be thus minded: and if in any thing ye be otherwise minded, God shall reveal even this unto you.

3. **Proverbs 24:3 (*TLB*)** — Any enterprise is built by wise planning, becomes strong through common sense, and profits wonderfully by keeping abreast of the facts.

GREEK WORDS

1. "now" — ἄρτι (*arti*): presently; at this present moment; here and now; right now

2. "we see" — βλέπω (*blepo*): to see, perceive, or discern

3. "through" — δι᾽ (*di*): pictures one trying to peer through something

4. "glass" — ἔσοπτρον (*esoptron*): a mirror made of highly polished metal; ancient mirrors were fashioned of highly polished metal so they could not produce a clear and distinct image; to get a better image, an onlooker had to look into the mirror from several different angles; here we see an ardent student looking at revelation from different angles or standpoints to try to get a clearer image of truth; also used to depict Roman glass

5. "darkly" — αἴνιγμα (*hainigma*): something that is obscure; where we get the word "enigma"

6. "then" — τότε (*tote*): then, at that precise moment

7. "now" — ἄρτι (*arti*): presently; at this very moment
8. "I know" — γινώσκω (*ginosko*): to know, perceive, or comprehend; to recognize
9. "in part" — ἐκ μέρους (*ek merous*): partially; from parts; pieces, not the whole picture
10. "perfect" — τέλειος (*teleios*): a full-grown adult; pictures one who is mature
11. "thus minded" — τοῦτο φρονῶμεν (*touto phronomen*): the word τοῦτο (*touto*) means this; the word φρονῶμεν (*phronomen*) is the plural form of φρονέω (*phroneo*), from φρήν (*phren*), and it describes one's mind or intellect; to focus or to fix one's thoughts on something; pictures a mental decision to refocus one's thinking
12. "otherwise minded" — ἑτέρως φρονεῖτε (*heteros phroneite*): the word ἑτέρως (*heteros*) means differently or even out of synch with the rest; the word φρονεῖτε (*phroneite*) is a form of φρονέω (*phroneo*), from φρήν (*phren*), describing one's mind or intellect; to focus or to fix one's thoughts on something; pictures a mental decision to refocus one's thinking; pictures one who thinks out of synch with the way he ought to be thinking or seeing a situation
13. "reveal" — ἀποκάλυψις (*apokalupsis*): something that has been veiled or hidden, but suddenly becomes clear and visible to see; a sudden revealing; to uncover; a veil is suddenly removed and what was once hidden comes into plain view; to see clearly what previously could not be seen

SYNOPSIS

Every year, just before the new year begins, Rick and Denise Renner gather with their top ministry leaders for a gut-level evaluation of everything they're doing. In attendance are individuals like Andrey Vasilyev, who leads the online Good News Church, which is a massive congregation of about 200,000 people. Also joining the discussion is Yura Ruls, who began working with the ministry in 1996. He oversees the media company that distributes the teaching of the Word of God throughout the length and breadth of the former Soviet Union, which extends across 11 time zones. Also present is Leonid Bondarenko, who joined the team in 1992 and initially served as the youth pastor of the church plant in Riga, Latvia. Today, he's in charge of all data for the online church. And last but certainly not least, is Paul Renner, who heads up the Moscow Good News

Church. Paul has been serving in some capacity of ministry since he was about two. He's a seasoned leader and tremendous asset to the team.

As Rick and Denise and their top ministry team members assemble, the first thing they do is *remember* what God has called them to do. Next, they each begin to *make a full review* of the facts of where they are in each area of ministry. The third step they take is to *make an honest report* about what they need to change and do differently in order to accomplish their vision. Fourth, they make a concerted decision to *revise* whatever methods are not working and begin implementing a new plan. This brings us to the fifth and final phase of starting the new year strong — *restructuring*.

The emphasis of this lesson:

The fifth step to starting the new year strong is to restructure. This means making adjustments in the way you think and willingly changing things in your life — such as your finances, your schedule, and your relationships — in order to faithfully fulfill God's calling.

A REVIEW OF OUR PREVIOUS LESSONS

To Start the New Year Strong…

1. Take time to REMEMBER the vision God gave you for your life.
2. Be willing to MAKE AN HONEST REVIEW of the facts of where you are and the progress you are making toward fulfilling your vision.
3. Then, MAKE AN HONEST REPORT to yourself, to the Lord, to your family, and to your team. This report reveals what you're doing right, what you're doing wrong, and what needs to change in order to achieve your goals.
4. Using the report you've made, determine what and how you need to REVISE in order to move forward toward carrying out your calling.

If You've Made a Mistake…

You are not alone. Each of us has experienced times in our lives when we misinterpreted what we were supposed to do. We were following the direction of the Holy Spirit as best as we could — sincerely believing we were supposed to do something, but we later discovered we misunderstood what God wanted us to do. This scenario is quite normal for believers. The apostle Paul addressed the cause for this phenomenon in First Corinthians 13:12, which says, "For now we see through a glass darkly.…"

'For Now We See Through a Glass Darkly'

We saw that the word "now" is the Greek word *arti*, meaning *presently*; *at this present moment*; *here and now*; or *right now*. Twice in the same verse, Paul spoke explicitly about our present, temporary life on earth. Here, he said, "Right now, at this present moment, we see things through a glass darkly."

The words "we see" is a translation of the Greek word *blepo*, which means *to see, perceive, or discern*. In this present life, there are some things we're able to see and understand. Yet there are times when we can't see things clearly — we see them "through a glass darkly." That is when we often make mistakes.

We learned that the word "through" is a translation of the Greek word *di*, and it *depicts one trying to peer through something that is hard to see through*. We also discovered that the word "glass" does not refer to a clear, modern-day window pane. It is the old Greek word *esoptron*, which describes *a mirror made of highly polished metal*. In the ancient world, mirrors were fashioned of highly polished metal, and they could not produce a clear and distinct image. To get a better glimpse of what was being looked at, the viewer had to look into the mirror from many different angles.

The word *esoptron* — translated here as "glass" — was also used to describe Roman glass. During biblical times, Roman glass was quite popular, but it was very flawed. Although its aqua blue color was very beautiful, it was only useful for allowing light to come into a room. In fact, if you wanted to see something through Roman glass, you had to peer long and hard to try and make out anything on the other side.

The apostle Paul used this word *esoptron* — glass — to depict an ardent student looking at revelation from several different angles or standpoints, trying to get a clear image of truth. Sometimes when we're trying to grasp the Word, it's like we're holding a hand mirror of highly polished metal trying to get clear understanding. We can see an image, but it's not distinct. Even after we look at it from several different angles, we still can't comprehend the meaning.

This brings us to the word "darkly," which is the Greek word *hainigma*. It describes *something that is obscure*. It is from where we get the word "enigma," which is the word for *a mystery*.

Through these words, Paul is letting us know that there are some things we just don't see clearly. We may have a general knowledge of something from Scripture, like it is God's will that we be healed or that He wants us to walk in prosperity. But seeing and experiencing His healing and prosperity are sometimes a real challenge. These situations are like looking through Roman glass that only lets us see bursts of light. We understand what God's will is in the Bible, but clearly seeing what to do to bring it about is a mystery. If we will listen to the Holy Spirit and allow Him to lead us, we'll make fewer mistakes. But as long as we're living on earth, we're going to see through a glass darkly, and it's likely we're going to make mistakes. It's important to note that the problem lies in our humanity — not with God.

'Now We Know in Part'

Paul went on to say, "…Now I know in part; but then shall I know even as also I am known" (1 Corinthians 13:12). The words "in part" is the Greek word *ek merous*, which means *partially* or *from parts*. It denotes *pieces, not the whole picture.* In other words, right now in this present, earthly life, we know *parts* or *pieces* about God and His will for our lives — we don't know the whole picture.

For example, when God first called Rick and Denise and their family to relocate to the former Soviet Union, Rick did not see the whole picture of what God wanted them to do. At that time, all he knew was that God was asking him to make a one-year commitment to move his family to serve in the former Soviet Union. That was the only "piece of the puzzle" he could see. It was small enough that he could embrace it and say yes to it.

Once he moved his family and they were living in the former Soviet Union, God then revealed the next piece. Rick began to understand that the commitment God was calling him and his family to make was not just for one year — it was a *lifetime commitment.* The truth is, sometimes God only shows us one piece of our life at a time because if we saw the whole picture, it would be too difficult for us to embrace — and it would probably scare us. The fact that He only shows us one piece at a time is actually an expression of His mercy.

As time passed, God unveiled the next piece of the calling on Rick and his family: He led them to begin ministering through television. Once they became obedient in that area, God revealed the next piece, which was to start a church and then multiple churches. The next thing God asked Rick to do was to take his TV ministry around the world and begin writing books. With each step of obedience, God showed Rick another piece of His will for him and his family. That is often how God works — He reveals things one piece at a time.

Sometimes when all you can see is one or two pieces of your life and you don't see the entire picture, your spiritual vision is blurred. Again, this is when you tend to make mistakes and misinterpret what God is asking you to do. If that has happened to you and you've deviated from God's plan for your life, repent and get back on track. Don't waste time wallowing in regret about past mistakes. If God has helped you better understand the assignment you received from Heaven, then begin moving in the right direction!

'Restructuring' Is All About Change

After you've reviewed the facts, made an honest report, and recognized what needs to be revised, the next crucial step to getting back on track to fulfilling your destiny is to *restructure*. Restructuring is all about change. Many times the methods and practices that worked in one season of our life will not work in the next. In order to reach your goals, you need to restructure or change things. Yes, sometimes restructuring is painful, but if you're going to do what God has called you to do, it is essential. This is where the rubber meets the road.

Now, saying you want to change and actually doing it are two different things. In many cases, the spirit is willing but the flesh is weak! You will know that you are really sincere and want to obey what God is prompting you to do when the moment comes that requires you to change — and you actually do it. The truth is, restructuring often requires big changes. For example, it may require a change in your...

- Financial priorities
- Personal assignments
- Scheduling of time
- Living space
- Relationships
- The "rank and order" of who has authority in your life

Unfortunately, many people see the need to restructure as an interruption, and while it certainly can be, we have to learn to see God's purpose in the changes He's leading us to make. In other words, restructuring has to lead somewhere or it's pointless and frustrating. If there's no concrete reason why restructuring is occurring — it becomes an event that just upsets everyone's world. But when we can see the positive direction it is taking us, we can work with it.

Researchers estimate that as many as 70 percent of all people do not like change. In fact, many of these individuals get very upset when restructuring takes place. For instance, when they are asked to change where they sit or move to a new desk at work, their world is turned upside down. If the boss asks them to shorten their lunch by fifteen minutes or come in a half an hour early for the next two weeks in order to expedite the completion of a project, they have a meltdown. Although these adjustments can be challenging, they are often necessary to attain greater productivity and move forward.

The bottom line: You can't keep doing things the same way and expect to get a better outcome. If you want new, better results, you need to restructure and use new and better ways. This means you have to be willing to embrace the vision God has given you and say, "Lord, I'm willing to make the changes I need to make in order to fulfill my purpose. I'm willing to adjust my daily schedule and routine, restructure my finances and priorities, and change my relationships and habits to do what You've called me to do. My greatest aim is to please You and be where You want me to be. Please show me what I need to do — one step at a time — to see that happen."

It's Time To Refocus Your Thinking and Fix Your Mind on God's Calling

Looking once more at Paul's letter to the Philippian believers, he said, "Brethren, I count not myself to have apprehended: but this one thing I do, forgetting those things which are behind, and reaching forth unto those things which are before, I press toward the mark for the prize of the high calling of God in Christ Jesus" (Philippians 3:13,14). This passage lets us know that Paul always had his God-given vision in front of him, and he was reaching for it and pressing toward it.

In the next verse, he went on to say, "Let us therefore, as many as be perfect, be thus minded: and if in any thing ye be otherwise minded, God shall reveal even this unto you" (Philippians 3:15). The word "perfect" is the Greek word *teleios*, which depicts *a full-grown adult* or *one who is mature*. The use of this word is the equivalent of Paul saying, "Let us therefore, as many as claim to be spiritually mature and thus minded...."

The phrase "thus minded" in Greek is *touto phronomen*. The word *touto* means *this*, and the word *phronomen* is the plural form of *phroneo*, which is from the word *phren*, and it describes *one's mind or intellect*. When these words are joined together to form *touto phronomen*, it means *to focus or to fix one's thoughts on something*; it pictures *a mental decision to refocus one's thinking*.

What was Paul instructing his readers to be "thus minded" about? The answer is in Philippians 3:14. He said to "...press toward the mark for the prize of the high calling of God in Christ Jesus." Paul focused his mind and fixed his thoughts on doing whatever he needed to do to accomplish God's call on his life, and he instructed everyone who is spiritually mature to do the same.

As You Seek God, He Will 'Reveal' to You What You Need To Restructure

Paul concluded Philippians 3:15 by saying, "...And if in any thing ye be otherwise minded, God shall reveal even this unto you." The phrase "otherwise minded" in Greek is *heteros phroneite*. The word *heteros* means *differently* or even *out of synch with the rest*; the word *phroneite* is a form of *phroneo*, which is from the word *phren*, describing *one's mind or intellect*, and it means *to focus or to fix one's thoughts on something*. When these words are joined together in this passage as *heteros phroneite*, it pictures *one who thinks out of synch with the way he ought to be thinking or seeing a situation*. Hence, anyone thinking differently must make a mental decision to refocus their thinking.

This brings us to the word "reveal," which is the Greek word *apokalupsis*. It describes *something that has been veiled or hidden, but suddenly becomes clear and visible to see*. This word denotes *a sudden revealing* and means *to uncover*. Furthermore, it depicts *a veil that is suddenly removed and what was once hidden comes into plain view.* It means to see clearly what previously could not be seen.

By using this word *apokalupsis* — translated here as "reveal" — Paul is saying, "God is so good and so desires to see you succeed that if you have any form of thinking that is out of sync and hindering you from fulfilling your calling, He will reveal it to you." When will God reveal the area, or areas, where your thinking needs to change? When you take time to *remember* His calling on your life, *review* the facts about where you are, honestly *report* your progress toward your vision, and determine what you need to *revise.*

Friend, God is not against you — He is for you! "What then shall we say to [all] this? If God is for us, who [can be] against us? [Who can be our foe, if God is on our side?]" (Romans 8:31 *AMPC*). As you work through the study and application questions for this lesson, humble yourself before the Lord and listen to the voice of His Spirit. What things has He been nudging you in your heart to change? What is He asking you to restructure in order to move forward and fulfill your destiny? If you are willing to change, He will empower you to change, and you will experience the blessings of being obedient!

STUDY QUESTIONS

**Study to shew thyself approved unto God, a workman that needeth not to be ashamed, rightly dividing the word of truth.
— 2 Timothy 2:15**

1. As you take steps to start the new year strong, what crucial instruction does God give you in Isaiah 43:18 and 19 to position you to move forward into His will? (Also consider Philippians 3:13.) Pray and ask Him to show you what things in your life fall into this category.

2. Restructuring can be a powerful catalyst to experiencing real, positive change. The key is in knowing *what* needs to change and *how* to change it. God made you and He holds the wisdom you need to know what you need to do at this stage of your life. Take a few moments to reflect on these verses and write down the essence of each promise God has made to you.

   • James 1:5

   • Psalm 32:8; Isaiah 30:21; 48:17

- Jeremiah 33:3
- Psalm 25:9,12-14
- Psalm 48:14; 73:24

PRACTICAL APPLICATION

**But be ye doers of the word, and not hearers only,
deceiving your own selves.
—James 1:22**

1. How do you normally respond to change (restructuring)? When you're asked to do things like adjust your work hours, redo something you've been working on, or even change the way you have been serving in ministry at your church, how do you tend to react? What is God showing you about your character through these situations?

2. The fact that God only shows us one piece of His will for our lives at a time is actually a blessing and an expression of His mercy. Stop and take a good look at where you are presently. Is there anything you're doing now that you're grateful God did not show you years ago? If yes, what is it, and why are you grateful He didn't show it to you earlier?

3. Take some time to stop and think: *What do I really want to accomplish in the next year? What do I want to see happen in my life, in the lives of my children/grandchildren, and with my job/business?*

4. Now pray, *"Lord, what do I need to do specifically to restructure in order to see these things become reality?"* Be quiet and listen. What action steps do you sense the Holy Spirit is asking you to take?

Notes